Era of Love

The Truth

Brandy Angel Wells

BookLeaf Publishing

India | USA | UK

Made with ❤ on the BookLeaf Publishing Platform
www.bookleafpub.in
www.bookleafpub.com

To God, whose unwavering love guides me every step.

To my parents, Janice and Larry, whose strength and sacrifice built the foundation of my dreams. To my life partner, Odanov, whose love is the light that inspires me to be my truest self.

And to my children, Felicity, Grace, Justice, and Princeton, who fill my heart with boundless joy and remind me daily what love truly means.

Thank you for showing me the epitome of true love.

Acknowledgments

Writing this book has been a journey of discovery, growth, and collaboration, and I am deeply grateful to all those who have supported and inspired me along the way.

First and foremost, I would like to thank my mother, Janice Wells, whose love, wisdom, and unwavering belief in me have been a constant source of strength. My father, Larry Wells, thank you for your encouragement and for always being there with advice and a listening ear. To my grandmother, Ruth Southerland, your life lessons and legacy have shaped me in more ways than I can count, and I am so grateful for your enduring influence.

I am blessed to have four incredible children—Felicity, Grace, Justice, and Princeton. Your joy, energy, and inspiration bring meaning to every day, and this book is dedicated to you. Your belief in me, even when I felt unsure, has kept me moving forward.

To my amazing husband, Odanov E. Martin, thank you for your endless support, your patience, and your love. You have been my rock throughout this process, and your faith in my work has meant everything to me. This book is as much yours as it is mine.

I would also like to thank my social media supporters, whose encouragement, feedback, and shared enthusiasm have been an incredible source of motivation. Your messages, comments, and insights have fueled me throughout this journey, and I am so grateful for each of you.

Finally, to my friends, colleagues, and mentors, thank you for believing in this project and for being there every step of the way. This book would not have been possible without your love, support, and guidance.

Thank you all from the bottom of my heart.

Preface

Era of Love is a poignant collection of poetry that invites readers on an intimate journey through the depths of the heart. Through verses that speak of passion, longing, joy, and sorrow, the author weaves an emotional tapestry that explores love's many facets and the pain that often accompanies it. From moments of bliss to the aching whispers of loss, this book transcends time and space, capturing the raw essence of human emotion. Era of Love is more than a collection—it is an exploration of what it means to love deeply and the transformative power of the heart.

Table of Contents

Era of Love

I walked through a doorway, broken and torn,
A heart full of grief, from love long worn.
Raised in a town where the fields met the sky,
But shadows of pain were too heavy to deny.
Generations of silence, abuse, and regret,
Where young girls were silenced, and love was
unmet.
Innocence stolen, with sneakiness and lies,
Neglect and betrayal, behind hollow eyes.

The weight of this curse, passed down through the
years,
Left scars on my soul and drowned me in tears.
Those who said they loved me, abandoned my
cries,
Leaving me broken, with no one to trust in their
lies.

Through nights filled with screams and days full
of pain,
I searched for the light to release me from the
chains.
And one quiet morning, I found something new,
A place full of promise, where the skies were blue.

The ruins of sorrow began to decay,
As I stepped into a brand-new day.
A new era beckoned, with a soft, steady hum,
Where love wasn't lost, but had finally come.
Blessed by God, with grace in my soul,
He lifted me gently, making me whole.
The universe whispered, in ways I could see,
The love I sought was always waiting for me.

In this era of love, I learned to be free,
To open my heart, to simply just be.
The wounds that scarred me, faded away,
As hope bloomed within me, day after day.
Now, love is not fleeting nor bound by the past,
But steady and sure, like the tide's gentle cast.
In this new place, I stand strong and aware,
For the era of love is mine to declare.

Saved

You talked to me, you cared for me, you comforted me, you loved me, you guided me, you confided in me, you chose me, you molded me, you gave to me, you touched me, you kissed me, you missed me, you made love to me, you sheltered me, you protected me, you proclaimed me, you never blamed me, you understood me, you took care of me, you held me, you shaped me, you had sight for me, you lifted me, you winged me, you flew with me, you stood by me, you were an angel to me, you gave heaven to me, you MADE me.

You hurt me, you hit me, you cheated me, you cheated on me, you deserted me, you abandoned me, you neglected me, you disrespected me, you misguided me, you slapped me, you tore me, you hated me, you cut me, you choked me, you did wrong by me, you faked me, you blew me, you chewed me, you spit me, you left me, you were cold-hearted to me, you ignored me, you walked away from me, you didn't miss me, you took from me, you shook me, you pulled me, you slung me, you were fake to me, you made a fool of me, you wronged me, you didn't care for me, you never loved me, you were hell to me, you broke me.

He found me, He carried me, He healed me, He took pain from me, He gave strength to me, He lifted me, He gave a gift to me, He died for me, He gave sight to me, He does right by me, He never left me, He looks over me, He's my inner beauty, He gave talents to me, He understands me, He stands by me, He sees for me, He leads me, He's my destiny, He gave love back to me, He gave a husband to me, He gave marriage to me, He blessed my family, He gave a dream to me, He makes my dreams true, He made me better for you, He loves me unconditionally, He holds me, He consoles me, He opened me, He gave prayer to me, gave His holy name to me.

In my heart for thee, I love He, because

He saved me.

Secrets of the Countryside

In the quiet fields where secrets sleep,
The country air holds stories deep.
Behind the trees and rolling hills,
Lies a truth that time can't still.
He was the shadow in the door,
A whispered name I'd heard before.
A smile so sweet, a voice so kind,
Yet in his eyes, a darker mind.
He watched through windows, cold and clear,
A silent stalker, filled with fear.
My innocence, a fleeting breath,
Caught in the hands of whispered death.
One day, he pulled me far inside,
To places no child should ever hide.
A room of silence, broken trust,
A stolen part, turned into dust.
He did the same to those I loved,

Under the guise of a family's blood.
But no one knew the pain we bore,
The secret cries behind the door.
When death took my mother, the truth unfurled,
Her absence made his lies swirl.
He said I wanted all of it,
A twisted claim to silence it.
Now the world thinks I am the one,
The wicked child, the evil spun.
But they don't see the tears I cried,
The soul I lost, the part that died.

Losing "it"

I was 12 when I truly lost it.
I almost had a fit.
It hurt so bad, I felt so sad; I ran a mile to escape
it.
But the truth was, it never really happened.
You can say I punked out. The moment it was
about to happen,
I tensed up and ran as fast as I could.
But I like to make myself believe it did happen.

I was 13 when I truly lost it.
I was getting out the tub and he took me in.
I said NO!! But he didn't hear, and he took it right
then.
Or was it a dream? I like to think so.
Therefore, it didn't really happen. Right?

I was 16 when I truly lost it. It was in a parked
church van.

In front of the church.
I squeezed, he screamed, and about 2 seconds later
it was over.
Really I didn't feel a thing.
I don't even know if it really happened at all.

I was 19 when I truly lost it.
My first love.
Could it really be happening?
I wanted to, and you did too, but right now I can't
remember.
Yeah we did do it, right?
I mean after all, we have a daughter to show for it.
I just can't seem to remember.

Locked In

I was just a child, but I knew the cold,
The deadbolt clicked, a story untold.
Windows nailed tight, no light would slip,
The silence pressed down with every grip.
She locked the phones, the remotes, the keys,
Her world was hers, while I begged for release.
Alone in the house, year after year,
A prisoner of silence, swallowed by fear.
Her boyfriend had a key, and with it, his claim,
A predator's eyes, a twisted game.
He came to me twice, hands I couldn't flee,
But I fought, I screamed, hoping someone would
see.
When I told her, her eyes turned cold,
Her silence, louder than words ever told.
She didn't believe me, dismissed all my cries,
Leaving me alone with terror in disguise.

I moved to protect myself, built walls so high,
A child forced to survive, to shield, to deny.
Her love was a lock, her care was a cage,
I learned to hide behind my own rage.
Now I look back, still haunted by those years,
The sound of that click, echoing in tears.
I grew strong from the pain I couldn't avoid,
But I still carry the silence, so paranoid.

Broken Soul

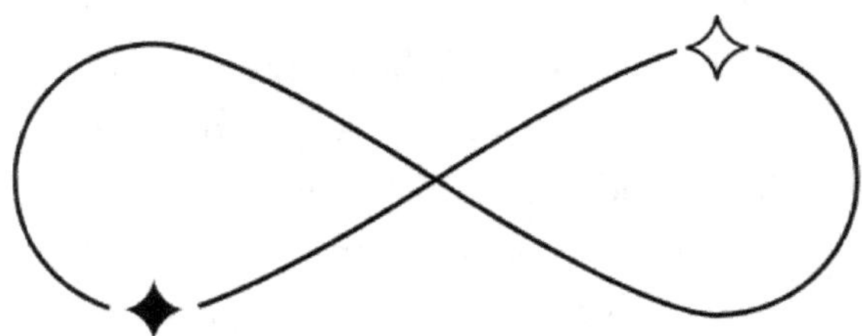

Thou held'st me near, but love was lost,
Thy hands, like storms, left hearts accosted,
And words like fire, they seared the night,
In quiet fury, I learned to fight—
Not with strength, but with retreat,
To hide, to shrink, to feel defeat.
When grief took root and tore thee apart,
It wast not only thy sorrow that broke my heart.

Mine, too, bled from the wounds thou mad'st,
A daughter lost, in thy coldness betrayed.
Bruised, misled, by the one I should trust,
I learned to hide, as love turned to dust.
I watched thee crumble 'neath the weight,
Of smoke, of drink, and all that pain.
Thine eyes grew dark, lost in thy rage,
And I, stuck in the middle, could not escape the

cage.

Thou wast a mirror, cracked and bent,
Showing all the scars thou ne'er meant.
I cried, I bled, but thou saw'st not,
Thou turn'd away and left me distraught.
The love I needed wast never there,
But empty bottles and silent despair.
I grew too strong, too numb to care,
Too weary to fix what wast not fair.

But then, when cancer came to claim,
God mended us, and we were not the same.
I miss thee now, though we found peace,
A daughter's love, forever released.
Now, I mourn not what we never had,
But the love thou couldst not give, and that makes
me sad.
But I rise, no longer afeard,
I've learned to let the light invade.
I miss thee, Mother, but in my soul,
I know we're healed, and I am whole.

Eleven

All I have left of you are 11 black stones of sadness.
My mind has moved, but my heart kept still.
This caused my feet to become paralyzed.
I just can't walk away from you.

What can I do to stop the pain?
I throw at you in hopes you will see my tears.
I yell to keep myself from dying.
I broke my own heart when I broke yours.

A song plays for you from my prayers to God.
You turn the music off.
I concentrate so hard on answers for our
problems.
But all I can see is what I feel. And what I feel is
that I love you.

I need you.
I need you because I love you.
I am in love with you.
But I feel as though it doesn't matter.

I don't know how to let these feelings go. Good or
bad.
I mess up every time. I lay next to you, and I feel
pain.
Pain, love, confusions, regrets, bittersweet feelings
of not being able to let go.
Moving forward, moving back, moving our bodies
in bed.
It's all an illusion of what we want to see.

Concentration is lost, yet I feel the need to think.
Then I can't seem to remember one single thought
I had.
I miss you, I miss us.
I miss the essence of being with you, happy.
I want you to be happy, even if I'm not.

I love you.

Just Another Day

Today was just another day, because you stole all
of my heart away.
You left me behind with a kiss in the wind.
I sit and wonder when my heart will beat again.
Every second goes by, and it seems I love you so
much more.
And surely know now it is you I adore.

I sit alone in my own silence, trying to control my
emotions, so my mind can be balanced.
I stay in solitude, and at the wall I stare, wishing
that it were you standing there.
I look in the mirror, and I see you in my heart,
and I wonder to myself, how is it that we are so
far apart. With tears in my eyes, I walk over to my
laptop, hoping for some mail.

Every time I start to read, hoping to see a
message, but every day it's nothing, and it feels
like hell.

Then I sit by the phone, hoping for a call from you
soon.
But of course nothing happens or it's never you.

Hold me, love me, want me, and need me, that's
all I need from you, you see, but day by day since
you left, I sit and dream of the day when you will
start back giving all your love to me.

Uncaged

Each morning, the alarm cuts deep. A sharp reminder of the life I keep. A cycle I can't break, no matter how I try. A constant pull that keeps me tied.

I stand before young minds each day, trying to light their path, show them the way, but inside, my fire is burning low. Trapped in a life where I cannot grow.

I sit in a classroom, my heart in pieces. As hours slip by, and the magic ceases. I give them my all, my energy, my soul. But I'm losing myself, and I'm far from whole.

The world outside, so bright, so wide. But here, I'm caged, nowhere to hide. I long to feel the wind on my face. To move, to breathe, to find my place.

Each lesson I teach, I pour out my heart. Yet still,
I feel I'm falling apart. These children, these teens,
they need me to be strong.
But I'm trapped in a place where I don't feel like I
belong.

I crave more than just a paycheck to live. I need to
break free, I need to forgive. Forgive myself for
the dreams I've denied. For the life I've put on the
other side.
How long can I ignore the ache inside? The fire to
explore, the urge to collide with a life that's mine,
that sets me free. Not bound by a classroom, but
by my own key.
I teach them to dream, to reach, to strive. Yet here
I am, trying to survive. Each day feels like another
disguise. A mask I wear, while my spirit dies.
I want to leave, to chase the air. To follow the
wind, and be truly there. I'm bound by these
walls, these lessons, this pace. In this cage where
my dreams have no space.
The clock ticks on, and so do I. A silent scream, a
desperate sigh.
But deep inside, I know it's true. One day, I'll
break free and start anew.

Threads Unwoven

When tales of strength were boldly spun,
Two souls entwined, their hearts as one.
A dance of love, a legacy born,
Mama's voice, a lullaby, worn.
Her touch, a balm, her laughter bright,
A spark of joy in the dead of night.
But time shifts, and shadows creep,
As dreams are met with eyes that weep.
Words once warm, now cold and still,
The silence is heavy, a bitter chill.
The kitchen hums with memory's weight,
A flicker of pride, a twist of fate.
The daughter's gaze, too proud to plead,
A quiet ache, a buried need.
Mama's eyes, sharp with untold grief,
Hold stories, sorrow's quiet thief.
Years of struggle, raw and deep,
The weight of survival, she must keep.
The daughter grows, bold and defiant,
With dreams too large, too cold, too reliant.

In silence, both stand, hearts entwined,
Two warriors bound, but love confined.
A glance, a breath, a chance to heal,
To find the strength, to love, to feel.
And maybe, once the storm has passed,
They'll see the love that will always last.

Burden of Silence

She stands at the edge of night, eyes wide, heart
clenched tight.
Outside, the moon bears witness, bold, to secrets
kept and stories untold. Mama's voice, a muted
song, warnings whispered, fierce and long: "Keep
this close, don't let them find, the things that
twist, the things that bind."
The secret weighs upon her chest, a burden that
never finds its rest.
Her days are spent in cautious steps, avoiding
glances, shallow breaths. Her friends laugh loud,
their worlds unscarred, their biggest fears, a test, a
card. They don't know what it's like to hold a pain
that cuts, a secret cold.
At school, her eyes are dark and guarded. Her
heart heavy, spirit broken, starved. Tired of being
Mama's shield. Her silence, her only field. The
world beyond her window calls, with promises of
freedom, no walls. She dreams of places, wide and

true. Where her voice can sing and not be
subdued.
"Why must I bear this weight alone?" Her heart
whispers, tired and torn. Mama's face, lined with
regret, haunts her soul, a deep-set debt. But the
girl aches for lands unknown, where chains are
broken, pain overthrown. Where laughter flows,
unforced wind,
Where she's not judged by what's within.
One step, then two, her breath is cold. The night
is fierce, the path is bold. She doesn't know where
she'll go, only that she's ready to let it show. A
prayer whispered to the stars, for freedom, peace,
and strength to fight. And though her heart still
aches and grieves,
The girl will run, the girl will leave.

Whispers in the Dark

She sits in shadows, quiet, small,
A child whose smile conceals it all.
Eyes too weary for her years,
Heart bruised by unshed tears.
Hands that hurt, voices that scar,
Memories buried, a wound too far.

A mother's strength, a father's fight,
Stories hidden, deep of night.
The whispers come, sharp and low,
Echoes of pain she won't let show.
No friends to lean on, no hand to hold,
Just the weight of secrets, heavy and cold.

Where color isn't both strength and stain,
Where she's not weighed down by this pain?
The world tells her to be tough, to stand,
To hide her hurt, to never demand.
But inside, she's a fragile thread,
A soul that longs for words unsaid.

And then, one night, in the silent ache,
A voice whispers, soft and awake.
A warmth, a light, a gentle grace,
A promise held in a sacred place.
"I see you, child, I know your heart,
I've walked this path, I've felt the start.
I made you strong, though you don't see,
Your pain will pass, but you'll be free."

A prayer that rises, raw and true,
A melody, old and new.
The girl who once stood on the brink,
Find a hand, a place to think.
In the quiet, in the soft and warm,
She feels His love, a shelter from the storm.
The storm subsides, the chains break loose,
A heart restored, a soul's truce.
No longer alone, no longer scared,
In His love, she is declared.

Echoes of Strength

I stand before the mirror, eyes meet mine,
A stranger's gaze, where battles intertwine.
The scars remain, the shadows stay,
Reminders of what I lost, what slipped away.
They say, "You're stronger now," but they don't know,
The moments I stumble, the fear I show.
A sudden sound, a touch, a word,
Releasing the storm, the memory stirred.
Triggers sharp as glass and steel,
Slice through peace, make me feel.
But I am learning, day by day,
To hold the mirror, come what may.
I'm more than my past, more than the ache,
More than the moments that made me break.
I am the sum of every scar I've known,
A warrior who stands, though I stand alone.
I'm allowed to have my cracks,

To feel the weight, to face what comes back.
Some days, the echoes win,
But I fight to stay, to breathe again.
When they point out every flaw,
I stand my ground, defy the law.
I speak to the girl in the mirror's eye,
And say, "I love you, I know why."
You're stronger than the nights that scarred,
Braver than the battles, the times you're marred.
You are more than they choose to see,
You are love, you are free.

Echoes of Goodbye

The house is still, too loud, too bare,
Echoes of laughter hang in the air.
Where hearts once beat, now silence screams,
A love now lost in broken dreams.
I trace the photos, fingers tremble,
Each smile is a lie, too sharp to handle.

He promised forever, love untold,
But in the quiet, the truth unfolds.
A room once shared now holds the pain,
Shattered dreams in a broken frame.
They tell me, "Be strong," but no one sees,
The nights I cry, the silent pleas.

He took the trust, the peace, the light,
Left me to fight, alone at night.
Accusations fly, cruel and cold,
But I rewrote the story told.
My heart, a battlefield, scarred and torn,
Yet in the rubble, I'm reborn.

I am more than the shame, the lies,
More than the past, more than the cries.
I rise above, my heart unbound,
A woman who fights, my voice resounds.
The silence now sings a healing tune,
A warrior's strength, a rising moon.

Let them talk, let them stare,
I've found my strength, I've found my air.
The love that once was, now a scar,
But I am more, I am the star.

And with each breath, I take my stand,
A life rebuilt by my own hand.
The journey's mine, the path I choose,
No longer bound, no longer bruised.

Echoes of Healing

In the silence where shadows loom,
In the corners of my broken room,
There's a voice that stirs the night,
A whisper calling, "You'll be alright."

Echoes of healing, tender and deep,
A balm for the wounds, for the soul's weep.
They come in moments, small and slight,
A glimmer of hope, a spark of light.

From nights of fear, from days of pain,
When I bore the weight, the loss, the shame,
A promise lingers, soft and true,
That I am more than what I've been through.

I hear it now, in the strength I find,
In the courage to leave the past behind.
The heart that beats, the breath I take,
The peace that blooms, the steps I make.

I was once chained, my spirit bound,
Trapped in the dark, where hope couldn't be
found.
But even shattered, even torn,
I moved forward, though weary and worn.

I listen close, for in this place,
Where tears have flowed and trials traced,
God's love has seeped into each scar,
Turning pain to light, each wound a star.

So when memories return and stir,
When doubt and hurt begin to blur,
I remember this, the truth I know,
Echoes of healing, deep and bold.

They sing of strength, they sing of grace,
A promise that time will heal every trace.
And in my heart, a song will rise,
A tale of survival beneath the skies.

Echoes of a Broken Vow

I stood before God, before friends and the skies,
With a ring on my finger and love in my eyes.
We promised forever, or so I believed,
A bond I cherished, a heart deceived.

You were my partner, my companion, my all,
Through seasons of laughter, through the rise and
fall.
But there were whispers I chose to ignore,
Hints of something hidden, something more.

Then came the morning, sharp and cruel,
A truth revealed, harsh and brutal.
A message on my phone, out of the blue,
A stranger's voice, telling me what you'd do.

"We met on Facebook, a chat that went too far,
A night of recklessness, a broken star.
He's married to you, but we shared that space,
A secret moment, a fleeting embrace."

A voice, a tremor, raw with rage,
The other lover, caught in betrayal's cage.
They, too, had been deceived, betrayed, and
shamed,
In the web of lies, we both were framed.

My knees gave way, my world collapsed,
The man I loved had tore me in half.
Grief sank deep, bitter and cold,
Unanswered questions, a tale left untold.

How do you heal when trust is broken,
When vows are shattered and words unspoken?
The truth was brief, yet its weight immense,
A fleeting weakness, a wound so intense.

For now, I carry lessons learned,
A heart once broken, now discerned.
I will love again, not as I did before,
But wiser, stronger, whole to the core.

Delulu

I was once delusional, led down a path of
unrighteous shame.
I was once out of my mind, thinking I would keep
his last name.
I laid my heart down in the instance of our
meeting of thine eyes.
He was single, no wife, no kids, my dumb ass
didn't even ask why.

I was once blinded by a love that felt so sweet,
But in my heart, I knew the truth—he was
incomplete.
I believed the lies that we told ourselves at night,
Drowned in promises that never saw the light.

How foolish was I to think he was the one,
When the signs were there, hidden under the sun.
His silence spoke louder than words ever could,
But I ignored it all, thinking I would be good.

I dreamed of the life we could've had,
But the reality was that I was just sad.
For in his eyes, I was nothing but a game,
And now I see clearly, I was never to blame.

The love I thought we shared was a fleeting
illusion,
A fleeting spark, lost in confusion.
I thought I could change him, make him whole,
But in the end, it was just my own soul.

Now I walk away, wiser from the pain,
No more false hope, no more feeling insane.
For I know my worth and won't play the fool,
I'll heal my heart and start living true.

Quiet Heart

Your laughter was the echo that filled my days,
Your voice, my anchor, my guide, my praise.
You were the light that chased away dark,
The steady flame, the brightest spark.
Then came the words, a cruel twist of fate,
A diagnosis that shifted my world's weight.
The battle that raged within your veins,
A war fought with courage, with unspoken pains.

I watched you, my mother, my friend, grow weak,
Your smile fading, your spirit on the brink.
I held your hand as it trembled in mine,
Praying for miracles, for more time.
I watched the days blur, the nights drag long,
Saying goodbye with every breath, every song.
And when that moment came, cold and deep,
The silence that followed, a wound I couldn't
keep.

The air was heavy, the room stood still,
My heart shattered, my voice lost its will.
The scent of you, the light you gave,
All left behind, a ghost, a grave.
I am your child, the lone, the only,
Carrying the weight, the grief, the lonely.
Your absence fills the hours, the dark, the dawn,
The quiet of a world now withdrawn.

I stand in the places where we shared,
Where your laughter lingered, where you cared.
Your voice is gone, but it echoes in me,
A part of my being, a part I can't flee.
I speak to the stars, I trace your face,
In memories, in dreams, in every space.
The world has moved on, and I must too,
But I carry you, every piece, every hue.

In the moments of doubt, in the storms I face,
You are there, a silent, guiding grace.
In the quiet, in the ache, in the silent room,
You live in me, forever, in the bloom.

Repeated Darkness

I thought I had learned, I thought I had grown,
Each scar a lesson, each loss a stone.
But love's cruel game, its sharp, heavy hand,
Pulled me back, deeper into the sand.
Another promise, another vow,
A chance at hope, a chance to allow
My heart to trust, my soul to believe,
That this time, this time, I'd not grieve.
But the weight came back, heavy and raw,
The silence of betrayal, the gnaw.

I fell, I stumbled, I lost my way,
Back into shadows where I used to stray.
The dark whispered secrets, cold and deep,
The pain of memories, the wounds I keep.
And there, in the chaos, in the sleepless nights,
I held the pieces, the broken fights.
A single mother, fierce and worn,
A warrior in the storm, battered and torn.

The weight of raising, the weight of care,
The nights I wept, the silent prayers.
For my children's smiles, for their peace,
For the hope that one day, this pain will cease.
I am both mother and mourner, both lost and
found,
In the quiet, in the noise, I seek the sound.
A voice that whispers, "You are more,
You are more than this, more than before."
Through the haze, I search, I reach, I find,
Fragments of courage, pieces of mind.

The dark may come, it may creep, it may stay,
But I'm here, I'm fighting, day by day.
With each sunrise, with each tear that falls,
I rise again, I answer my calls.
For the dark may come, and the pain may linger,
But in my heart, there's a flicker, a figure.
The strength that carried me, the love that shines,
The light that's mine, in all my lines.

Unsuspecting Love

I had sworn it, said it fierce and loud,
Carved in the silence, in the pain I'd allowed.
Never again, I'd told my mirror's face,
No more heartache, no more love to chase.

Life had taught me lessons, terribly harsh and raw,
A love that left me empty, many bonds falling
apart
Where hope was a gamble and trust a rare find,
I shut my heart down and left it behind.

But there you were, eyes like indefinite fire,
A spark in the dark, a sweet quiet desire.
A laugh that cuts through the night's deep,
A warmth that woke me from my sleep.

How did this happen, this twist of fate?
Another chance when I'd closed the gate.
The scent of freedom, the beat of a song,
A feeling that told me I had been wrong.

I told myself here, I'd never return,
To that place where my heart would yearn.
Where love was a gamble, a battle untamed,
Where hearts broke and hope was maimed.

But your voice, so smooth, so deep, so true,
Pulled me out from the shadows, slowly into you.
Your touch, strong and familiar, but new,
Reopened doors I thought I'd painfully outgrew.

We were two souls, scarred and worn,
From the battles fought, from nights we mourned.
But here, in the noise and in the quiet space,
A love so deep, it showed me grace.

So here I stand, under the starlit sky,
Where love was a word, now a sigh.
With eyes wide open, heart raw, still bruised,
Finding in you, a love I never knew.

Unresolved Triggers

I sit in the quiet, the stillness of night,
Where shadows dance and stars take flight.
The weight of old wounds, the ache of the past,
A heartbroken girl but longing to last.

I call out to the silence, praying on my knees,
Where secrets and sorrows lie and sadness seep.
"Let me mend, let me heal, let me find
The strength to leave these old hurts behind."

This love, so new, so fierce and bright,
Deserves more than the depth of night.
It deserves the fullness of my heart,
A tender gift, a fresh start.

I whisper to God, to the moon's soft glow,
"Help me heal, help me grow.
I want to be whole, for him, for me,
To love freely, to finally be free."

Can the past be a lesson, a page now turned,
Can the embers of hope once more be burned?
I want to stand, strong and true,
A woman reborn, ready for you.

Help me release the doubts that cling,
The scars that still sting, the shadows they bring.
Let me be open, let me be brave,
Let me be the woman you'll love, the woman you
crave.

This new love, so precious, so rare,
Deserves all of me, my soul laid bare.
So heal me, heart, heal me, soul,
Restore me, and make me whole.

With each breath, with each prayer,
I gather courage, I shed despair.
For this love, for this chance to see,
The woman I'm meant to be, finally free.

The Lies He Told

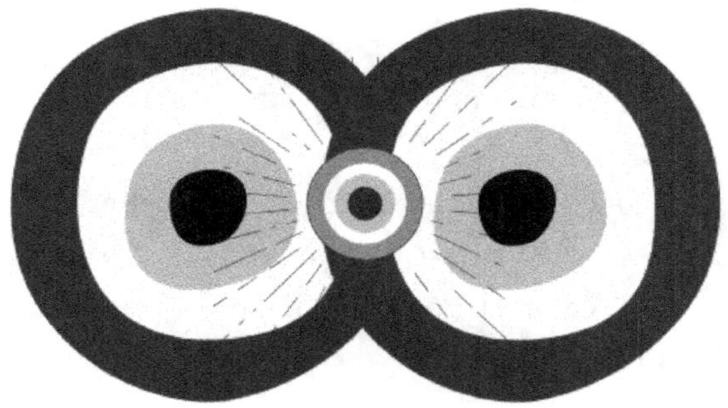

He wore a mask of love, a careful lie,
But behind it, deceit was clear in his eyes.
A serial cheater, a master of games,
Leaving scars on my soul, burning my name.
He tore me down with words so cruel,
A verbal storm, a twisted fool.
I caught him time and time again,
With other women, lies, and sin.
He stalked my steps, threatened my peace,
Lied to the law, hoping my hurt would increase.
He painted me evil, while he wore a crown,
Ripping my soul, trying to break me down.
In court, he lied, called me unfit and vile,
Said I was a danger, with a wicked smile.
He painted false pictures, a mission to destroy,
My motherhood, my peace, my sanity, my joy.

When he and his wife took my children, my heart
froze,
No remorse, no shame, just chaos he chose.
I fought back, tracked them down,
A mother's strength knows no bounds.
When they kidnapped them, I feared for their
soul,
A nightmare I lived, spun out of control.
I tracked my daughter's phone, took action fast,
I wasn't going to let his evil terror last.
He called the cops again, spun his tale,
Said he feared for his life, made me frail.
They took me away, locked me tight,
For 24 hours, I faced the night.
But when I walked out, I didn't break,
I fought for my children, for their sake.
I hired a lawyer, took back what was mine,
I'm reclaiming my strength, one step at a time.

A Letter to My Rays of Sunshine

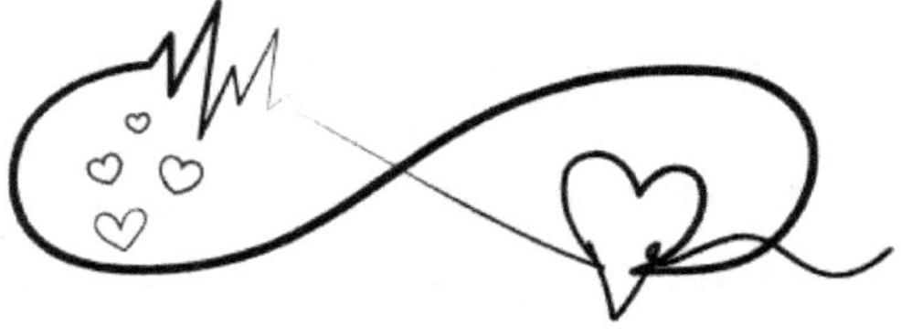

Forgive me, for the times I fell,
For moments I couldn't break the spell
Of doubt and pain that clouded my way,
And in those shadows, I couldn't stay.
I'm sorry for the nights of endless tears,
For hidden fears and unspoken years,
When my heart ached but I couldn't show,
The love that effortlessly and fiercely would grow.
The failed vows, the broken dreams,
The pains of the past, or so it seems,
They carved their tale, left marks on me,
Yet through it all, you set me free.
You are the light that calls me home,
The reason I am never alone.
I know I've stumbled, I've made mistakes,
Choices that bent but never broke the stakes.
I've learned love's more than words we say,

It's a promise kept, a lighted way.
I will be here, through every storm,
A steady hand, a heart that's warm.
To hold you close, to lift you high,
To see the world through your bright eyes.
For in your laughter, I find my song,
In your courage, I am strong.
You are my reasons, my hope, my why,
The dream I chase, the wings I fly.
I promise this, through each day's end,
To be your mother, your fiercest friend.
Thank you for patience, for your trust,
For loving me, imperfect and just.
I am so proud, so blessed, so true,
There's no greater gift than the gift of you.

Keep it Between Us

In the light of day, we made our vow,
Under sunlight's glow, beneath the sky's brow.
No grand celebration, no crowd to see,
Just you and me, where we're meant to be.
A secret held, a sacred keep,
A prayer God answered, a love so deep.
I caught your gaze, and my heart skipped,
A warmth so fierce, a fire lit.
Your hand in mine, a touch so true,
In that moment, the world faded to you.
We chose to guard this precious flame,
To keep it safe, to keep it tame.
Only hearts close, the ones who know,

Will share in what we've come to show.
In stolen glances, in the laughter we share,
In whispered words, in the way we care.
The world may wonder, the world may guess,
But this love is divine, it's ours to bless.
The days will pass, the seasons will turn,
We'll wait for the time when others learn.
For now, it's just us, this secret we keep,
A promise made, vows to reap.
In the warmth of sun, in the light of noon,
We cherish the life we've built so soon.
When the world's ready, when the moment is
right,
We'll share our love, in the full of light.
But for now, in this sacred time,
I hold you close, heart and mind.
A marriage of hearts, a love so true,
A treasure hidden, shared by just a few.
In your arms, my heart finds peace,
A love that never asks for release.
With every beat, with rings held high,
You are my forever, my reason why.

Dear Adversary

You tried to break me, You tried to tear me apart,
Throwin' stones at my soul, but I still got heart,
You thought you'd silence me, put me in the
ground,
But one monkey won't stop my show, it's still
going down.
I been through the fire, came out strong and bold,
Like alchemy, I turned my pain into solid gold.
You tried to crush me, make me feel small,
But I'm built to last, I rise above it all.
You hit me with hate, but I'm surrounded with
light,
The Lord's my shepherd, and I'm ready for the
fight.
You tried to tear me down, but I found my flow,
I'm a survivor, I'm a queen, and I'm ready to grow.

You tried to block me, but I came back stronger,
I'm the whole forest, baby, I have a whole new
hunger.
I turned my wounds into wisdom when all I had
was hope,
With God on my side, I'm on a mission for my
soul.
You thought you'd keep me down, thought you
had the key,
But I broke the chains, now I'm flying free.
No longer a prisoner of your lies or deceit,
I'm rising from the ashes, a healed soul complete.
You pushed me down in the fire, thought I'd burn
out,
But like Shadrach, Meshach, I stand without
doubt.
You can't stop me, I'm blessed and redeemed,
God's got my back, no weapon formed against me.
In the pain you caused me, you made me rise,
Taught me to fight with fire in my eyes.
You tried to tear me down, but I'm standing tall,
Now I'm walking in my power, I'm unstoppable!
So, thank you for the lessons, all the pain you
caused,
It made me who I am, no apologies, no pause.
You tried, but you failed, yeah, you didn't win,
I'm walkin' in faith, let the healing begin.

Shadows

I saw the demons in the night,
Whispers cold, a chilling bite.
Their eyes burned red, their claws stretched wide,
They crept inside, nowhere to hide.
In my sleep, they'd paralyze,
Their icy grip, my waking cries.
Nightmares danced beneath my mind,
Tormenting shadows, cruel and blind.
I fought with fury, broken, torn,
Through endless nights and nights of scorn.
But in the dark, I called His name,
And God descended, fierce as flame.
The demons snarled, they tried to cling,
But His light shattered everything.
With every step, they lost their hold,
Their screams grew faint, their hearts grew cold.

I battled on with God at my side,
Through nightmares that would not subside.
His power burned, a sword so bright,
That pierced the darkness, brought me light.
Now I walk, no fear to keep,
No paralyzing grip in my sleep.
The demons quiver, their strength undone,
For God has triumphed, and I have won.

Self-Doubt

I look in the mirror, and I feel so ashamed.
I have mastered being the one to blame.
I am not good enough so I say,
But deep inside I know I can find a way.
But here I am again, lost, no will
My mind goes against the way I feel.
I must challenge these shadows of doubt
I must get my head out of dark clouds.
I wallow in self-pity, stuck in the past
Chained to f.e.a.r., too distraught to last.
I try as I may, I push and I pull, I cry
I stumble to my knees, I feel I want to die.
On my knees, I feel a presence near,
I hear, my child please have no fear.
For you are mine, and mine alone.

For I am with you, your faith is sown.
I will carry you when you are not strong,
I will carry you even when the distance is
long.
I have heard your cries I have heard your
prayers
And you knew in your heart that I'd be there.
So when there's a doubt, know in your heart
That self-love will set you apart.
Feeling love for yourself may feel new,
But it reflects all the love I have for you.
***Written by Angel & Odanov

Era of Love Defined

The era of love is a journey divine,
Where hearts are lifted and spirits align.
It's finding God's embrace and living where love
shines.

Anew

I step into the dawn, leaving my shadows behind,
My heart reborn, in hope and love intertwined,
A future uncharted, my life redesigned.

Forgiveness

Hate once seethed, a poison in my veins,
A wound that festered, fed by silent pains.
Now it fades, leaving peace in its wake.

Love Reborn

A heart heals in time,
Wounds fade, new light softly grows
Love blooms once again.

Love after Him

I rise from wounds that once cut deep and wide,
In my own arms, I find the strength to heal,
Now self-love blooms where empty hurt once
tried.

The Passion We Share

In his arms, fire sparks with every touch,
Whispers of desire, we feel the rush,
A love so fierce, it burns and won't let go.

The Soliloquy of My Heart

As the rivers flow within the moments of pleasure, I long for thee.

He, who comes like a thief in the day, bold and brave. Accepting no defeats of love. His strengths make me surrender all that I own. He has the faith of the 12 disciples. The strength of the lion's den.

I cannot stray. I am energized by the mere sight of him. My soul spells out his name.

Only he can immense this pull of gravity on my heart.

Daring to fall in love with a wounded woman.

A man of absolute truth.

Never straying from the battle of healing the souls that were harmed.

Obedient as a servant of his destiny, leading, protecting, providing.

Visions of all that will be. To dream of a life

unlike anything of familiarity is of a dream.

Oh, how he weaves the light of hope into the dim corners of my heart, where shadows once danced with abandon. He stands as a lighthouse against the storm of doubt, a steady flame that reassures me there is no challenge he cannot face. His love speaks through actions, strong yet tender, a promise of safety and peace. In his embrace, I find the resolve to heal, and with his touch, I feel the weight of his unbreakable oath.

He is the architect of my new dawn, lifting me from the ruins of old scars and shaping me into a woman reborn by love's fire.

No longer haunted by the past, I am ready to embrace this rare gift. My heart beats to the rhythm of a future shaped by him, the man who is both my sanctuary and the dream I never dared to envision.

Together, we build a life beyond our pasts,
a legacy of love and purpose, rooted in truth and unshakable. With him, love is not fleeting but eternal, an ongoing hymn sung in both joy and vulnerability. Hand in hand, we step forward, beginning a journey that is not just extraordinary, but a testament to love's healing power.

Conclusion

As I reflect on this journey—through the pain, the growth, and the moments of profound clarity—I realize that love, in its purest form, is the alchemy that transforms everything. The lessons I've learned, the wounds I've healed, and the truths I've unearthed have all led me to one undeniable conclusion: that love is the force that connects us all, and through it, we find our power.

In sharing these poems, these untold stories, I've come to understand that vulnerability is not a weakness, but a strength. It is in embracing our deepest pain and transforming it that we find our true voice, and in turn, offer something to the world that can heal, inspire, and awaken others. To all those who have walked with me through these pages, I thank you for your courage to witness, to reflect, and perhaps, to see yourself in my words. I hope that through this book, you too find the courage to share your story, to speak your truth, and to know that your voice holds the power to change lives.

In the end, we are all on a journey toward love—toward understanding, compassion, and connection. If you've walked this path with me, I leave you with this: the pain is never permanent, the lessons are always valuable, and love is always the answer.

We are all here for a reason, and our stories matter. So, let your heart speak, and may it echo through the generations to come. The Era of Love is now, and it is ours to shape.

Community Work

A portion of the proceeds from Era of Love will be donated to the Kings & Queens Foundation, located in Columbus, GA. The Kings & Queens Foundation is a network dedicated to fostering success among young adults through the creative arts, including visual art, dance, theater, film, music, and other artistic endeavors. The foundation's mission is to provide a structured platform, resources, and guidance to individuals, especially those who are homeless, from low-income backgrounds, or at risk. By empowering these individuals with access to opportunities that promote personal and professional development, the foundation strives to improve their social and economic outcomes. Through this support, we hope to help foster a new generation of creators, dreamers, and leaders.

For Bookings and Public Appearances

For inquiries regarding bookings, public appearances, or any other professional engagements, please contact my agent at:
EraOfAngel@gmail.com

The Art of Surrender coming soon. It will
take you on an erotic
journey through a poet's mind.